I CAN READ
KINDERGARTEN READER

Seton Press
1350 Progress Drive
Front Royal, VA 22630
Phone: (540) 636-9990
Fax: (540) 636-1602

ISBN: 978-1-60704-171-9

Illustrated by Nathan Puray

For more information, visit us on the web at
www.setonpress.com

TABLE OF CONTENTS

A LAKE

We go up a hill.

We take Bud.

We take a pole.

We see a lake.

We see a bug.

We sit on a log.

We see a fin.

The End

THE BEE

The mule can
see a bee.

The bee can see the
mule. Go, mule, go!

The fox can
see the bee.

The bee can see the fox. Go, fox, go!

The pup can
see the bee.

The bee can see the pup. Go, pup, go!

Kate can
see the bee.

The bee can see
Kate. Go, Kate, go!

The End

CAN YOU?

Mike can dive.
Can you dive?

Mike can ride.
Can you ride?

Mike can hide.
Can you hide?

Mike can bike.
Can you bike?

Mike can hike.
Can you hike?

Mike can rake.
Can you rake?

Mike can bake.
Can you bake?

Mike can pop up.
Can you pop up?

Mike can hug a pup.
Can you hug a pup?

The End

AT HOME

We are on a hill.

We can see Fen.

We can see Len.

You are a cute
bug, Fen.

You are a cute
mole, Len.

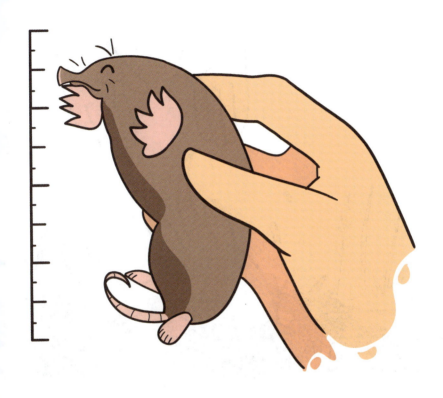

You are not tall.
You can go in a hole.

Go in the hole, Len.

Go in the hole, Fen.

You are at home.

The End

AN APPLE

I see an apple.

The pig can
see an apple.

The fox can
see an apple.

The yak can
see an apple.

An apple can
feed a yak.

An apple can
feed a fox.

An apple can
feed a pig.

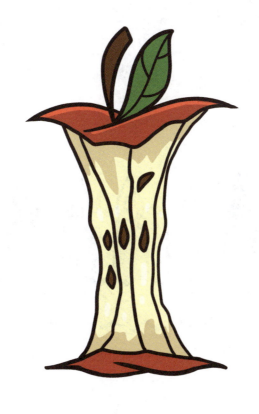

An apple can
feed me!

The End

THE CAKE

Luke and Joe
see Jane.

Can we make a cake, Jane?

Jane can make
the cake.

Luke and Joe can
mix the cake.

Can we bake
the cake?

Mom can bake
the cake.

Luke and Joe and
Jane like the cake.
Mmm! Mmm!

The End

I am a cat on a mat.

I am a hen in a pen.

I am a bug in a jug.

I am a mole in a hole.

I am a bat in a hat.

I am a pup in a cup.

I am a pig in a wig.

I am a fox in a box.

I am an ape in a cape.

The End

NEW WORD LIST

A Lake
a
Bud
bug
fin
go
hill
lake
log
on
pole
see
sit
take
up
we
The End

The Bee
bee
can
fox
Kate
mule
pup
the

Can You?
bake
bike
dive
hide
hike
hug
Mike
pop

rake
ride
you

At Home

are
at
cute
Fen
hole
home
in
Len
mole
not
tall

An Apple

apple
an

feed
I
me
pig
yak

The Cake

and
cake
Jane
Joe
like
Luke
make
mix
Mom

I Am

am
ape

bat
box
cape
cat
cup
hat
hen
jug
mat
pen
wig